Contents

Some words are shown in bold, **like this**. You can find out what they mean by looking in the Glossary.

Now you see it, now you don't!

People are always excited by magic. The most amazing tricks are based on skill and lots of practice. With a little work and a dash of **showmanship**, anyone can be a magician.

Try This At Home!

Fun Magic Tricks

Nick Hunter

4690565151 5

Raintree is an imprint of Capstone Global Library Limited, a company incorporated in England and Wales having its registered office at 7 Pilgrim Street, London, EC4V 6LB – Registered company number: 6695582

To contact Raintree please phone 0845 6044371, fax + 44 (0) 1865 312263, or email myorders@ raintreepublishers.co.uk. Customers from outside the UK please telephone +44 1865 312262.

Text © Capstone Global Library Limited 2013
First published in hardback in 2013
Paperback edition first published in 2014
The moral rights of the proprietor have been asserted.

Edited by Rebecca Rissman, Daniel Nunn, and Adrian Vigliano
Designed by Cynthia Della-Rovere
Picture research by Elizabeth Alexander
Production by Alison Parsons
Originated by Capstone Global Library Ltd
Printed and bound in China by China Translation and Printing Services Ltd

ISBN 978 1 406 25103 6 (hardback)
16 15 14 13 12
10 9 8 7 6 5 4 3 2 1

ISBN 978 1 406 25110 4 (paperback)
17 16 15 14 13
10 9 8 7 6 5 4 3 2 1

British Library Cataloguing in Publication Data
Hunter, Nick.
Fun magic tricks. -- (Try this at home!)
793.8-dc23
A full catalogue record for this book is available from the British Library.

Acknowledgements
We would like to thank the following for permission to reproduce photographs: Alamy p. 4 (© Bob Daemmrich); © Capstone Publishers pp. 5, 6, 7 t, 7 b, 9 t, 9 b, 10 t, 10 b, 11, 12, 13, 14 t, 14 b, 15 t, 15 b, 16, 17 t, 17 b, 18 t, 18 b, 19 t, 19 b, 20, 21 t, 21 b, 22 t, 22 b, 23, 24, 25 t, 25 b, 26, 27, 28, 29 (Karon Dubke); SuperStock p. 8 (© Blend Images). Design features reproduced with the permission of Shutterstock (© alphaspirit), (© Subbotina Anna), (© Four Oaks), (© Gelpi), (© Merve Poray), (© Nicemonkey).

Cover photograph of a magician reproduced with permission of iStockphoto (© Chepko Danil).

Every effort has been made to contact copyright holders of any material reproduced in this book. Any omissions will be rectified in subsequent printings if notice is given to the publisher.

All the internet addresses (URLs) given in this book were valid at the time of going to press. However, due to the dynamic nature of the internet, some addresses may have changed, or sites may have changed or ceased to exist since publication. While the author and publisher regret any inconvenience this may cause readers, no responsibility for any such changes can be accepted by either the author or the publisher.

Every magician needs some basic equipment, such as a magic **wand** and a table covered with a cloth that goes down to the ground.

Trick tip

The tricks in this book use everyday equipment. Some magic tricks use special equipment and can be dangerous. Be careful before you try anything too complicated.

That's knot magic!

Level of difficulty: Easy

Amaze your friends with a very simple rope trick.

STEP 1

First, find a piece of rope about a metre long. Ask your friends to make a knot without letting go of each end.

Trick tip

You can make even simple tricks more exciting by putting on a show. Keep chatting with your **audience**, so that they aren't looking at what your hands are doing.

STEP 2

When they admit defeat, fold your arms with one hand under your arm. Pick up one end of the rope in each hand.

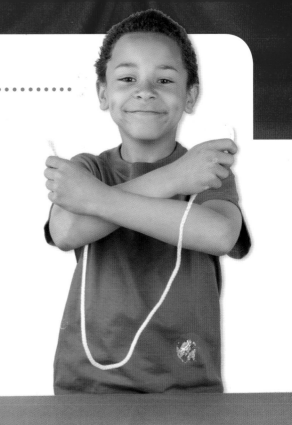

STEP 3

Pull the ends and **reveal** the magic knot.

Making money

A great magician can make something appear that wasn't there before, such as a rabbit from a hat.

You can start by making money appear from nowhere. Show the **audience** your hands, to show that they are empty.

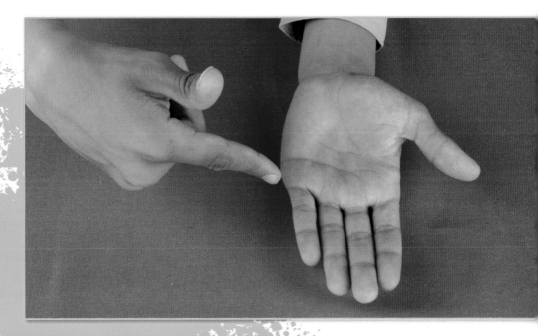

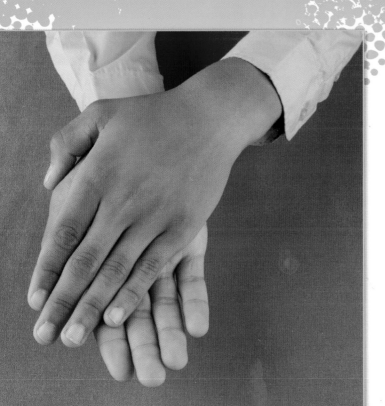

Then, rub your hands together and open them to **reveal** a coin in the palm of one hand.

Your friends will love your coin trick, but how is it done?

STEP 1

Hold a coin in your palm and bend your fingers slightly, so the flesh of your palm will grip the coin while looking normal.

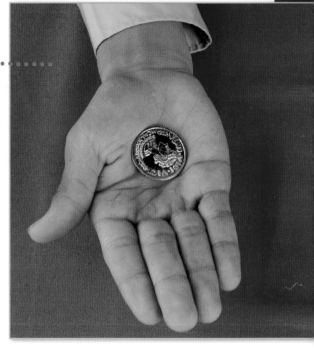

STEP 2

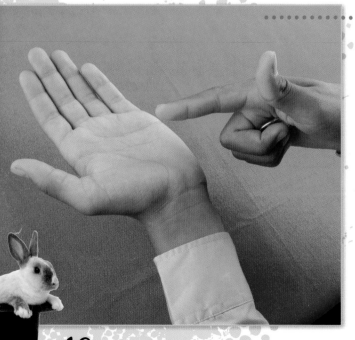

Very quickly, show that your hands are empty by pointing with the other hand. Your pointing fingers will hide the coin.

You can then reveal the coin.

Trick tip

Try holding a coin in your palm as you go about your normal day, so that it looks natural and you get used to the feeling.

Into thin air

As well as making things appear, magicians have to make things disappear. You'll be a hit at parties when you make a glass disappear.

Cover the glass with your (clean) handkerchief.

Then, lift it and slam it down on the table. Your **audience** will expect a big crunch, but instead, the handkerchief will be empty. The glass has vanished.

Trick tip

When you first try this trick, make sure you use a plastic cup that won't break.

This trick is all about preparation.

Cut out a disc of cardboard the same size as the top of the glass. Stick it inside a handkerchief or napkin.

STEP **1**

STEP **2**

Put your handkerchief over the glass and lift it towards you.

STEP 3

When you reach the edge of the table, drop the glass into your lap (or onto something soft). The card disc will make it look like the glass is still under the handkerchief.

STEP 4

Slam your hand down. It looks like the glass has disappeared!

Trick tip

Never show a trick to other people until you have tried it many times to make sure it's going to work.

Card sharp

A pack of **playing cards** is an essential tool for any good magician. There are thousands of great tricks you can do with a pack of cards.

Trick tip

Never show a trick twice to the same people. They're more likely to work it out the second time.

Pick a card

With this trick, your **audience** will believe that you can read minds. Ask one of them to pick a card from the pack and remember it.

The card is put back, and the pack is shuffled. Amazingly, you reveal the card that they picked. How is that possible?

Before your show, arrange all the cards in a pack into two halves so that all the cards with red and black **symbols** are grouped together.

Make sure your helper replaces the card in the opposite half of the pack than the one they took it from.

STEP 3

Take half the cards. Put them on the table and place the other cards on top. Do this **cut** several times to show that you are mixing the cards up.

STEP 4

Look at the cards. One card should be surrounded by cards of a different colour. Mystery solved!

Predict the card

Try predicting the card your **audience** will choose. Place a card on top of the pack, and write its name on a piece of paper.

STEP 1

Ask a helper to take a quarter of the cards, turn them face up, and put them back on the pack.

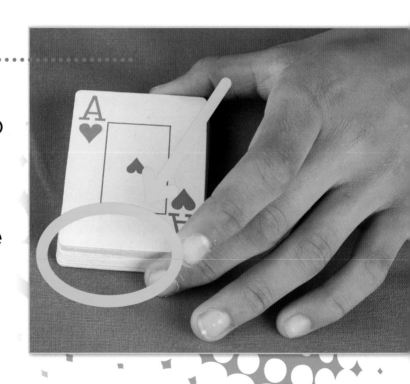

Next, ask them to take half the cards from the top of the pack and turn them over.

Fan out the cards, with the top one on the left. Ask your helper to pick the first face-down card.

Amaze them by showing that you already knew which card they would choose.

Mind reader

Some of the most amazing tricks happen when the magician appears to read the **audience's** mind. You'll need an assistant to help you with this one.

Your helper should pretend to be an ordinary member of the audience.

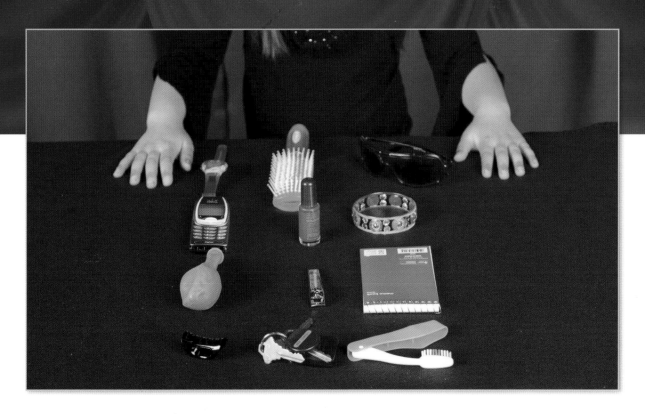

Select 12 personal items from your audience, including a phone with a keypad. If no one gives you a phone, have one of your own ready to use.

Trick tip

Most of the greatest magicians work with an assistant. This means you can do even more exciting tricks.

STEP 1 Leave the room and ask someone to select one of the items. They should hold it up, so that the **mind-reading** magician can sense it.

Audience members mix up the objects on the table. You reappear and ask your secret helper to point to each object in turn.

STEP **3**

You concentrate hard to pick up the mind waves. Finally, you select the right object. How did you do that?

This trick does not really rely on **reading minds**. The phone is the key.

When the person selecting the object holds it up, your helper can see it. The objects are arranged like a phone keypad: in four rows of three objects each.

When your hidden helper points to each object in turn, they touch the key on the phone's keypad that matches the chosen object's position.

Trick tip

Don't rush it. The longer you take, the more difficult the trick looks.

Showtime!

Now that you know some tricks, put it all together into a show for your friends and family. Make sure you have all the right **props**, such as a wand and a pack of cards.

Think about what you're going to say during the show. A skilled magician can make the simplest tricks exciting by telling jokes and having fun with the **audience**.

Trick tip

Never show how a trick is done. Once your audience sees how easy some tricks are, they won't be so impressed.

Glossary

audience group of people who come to see or hear a show

cut mix up cards by splitting the pack in half

mind reading finding out what someone is thinking without them telling you

playing cards pack of cards used for games or tricks. Each pack includes 52 cards made up of four different groups, or suits. Each suit has 13 cards numbered 1 to 10 and three picture cards (jack, queen, and king).

prop object used as part of a show or magic act

reveal show or uncover

showmanship making a show exciting for the audience

symbol sign or picture that means something

wand stick used by magicians to perform tricks

Find out more

Books

Card Tricks (Secrets of Magic), Stephanie Turnbull (Watts, 2011)

Magic Tricks to Make and Do, Ben Denne (Usborne, 2007)

Sleight of Hand (Magic Handbook), Joe Fullman (QED, 2008)

Websites

www.activitytv.com/magic-tricks-for-kids
This site features a selection of videos explaining how to do magic tricks.

www.kidzone.ws/magic
This site features magic tricks and tips on how to become a magician.

www.youngmagiciansclub.co.uk
The Young Musician's Club is a branch of the Magic Circle, the society for real magicians.

Index